PIANO DUET

1 PIANO/4 HANDS

HEART AND SOUL
& OTHER DUET FAVORITES

This publication is not for sale in the EU.

ISBN 978-0-634-05727-4

HAL•LEONARD®
CORPORATION

7777 W. BLUEMOUND RD. P.O. BOX 13819 MILWAUKEE, WI 53213

Visit Hal Leonard Online at
www.halleonard.com

HEART AND SOUL

& OTHER DUET FAVORITES

ANY DREAM WILL DO
from JOSEPH AND THE AMAZING TECHNICOLOR®DREAMCOAT

SECONDO

Music by ANDREW LLOYD WEBBER
Lyrics by TIM RICE

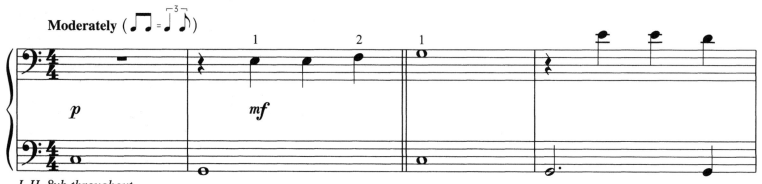

ANY DREAM WILL DO

from JOSEPH AND THE AMAZING TECHNICOLOR®DREAMCOAT

PRIMO

Music by ANDREW LLOYD WEBBER
Lyrics by TIM RICE

SECONDO

PRIMO

SECONDO

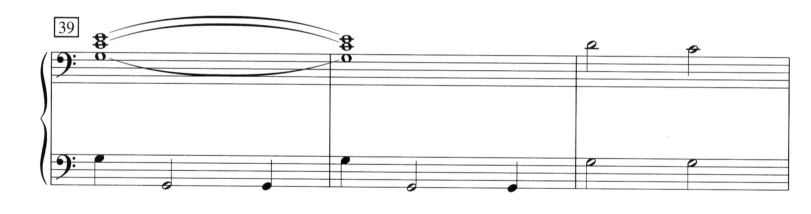

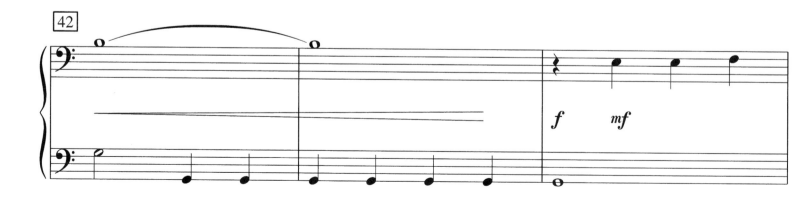

PRIMO

SECONDO

PRIMO

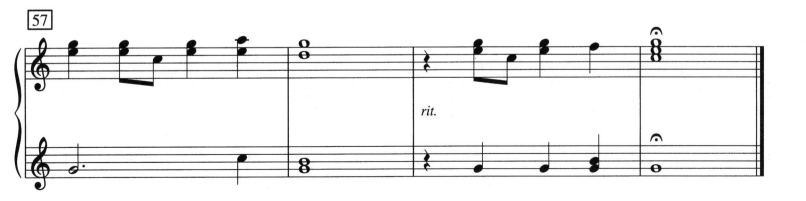

CHOPSTICKS

By ARTHUR DE LULLI

SECONDO

Brightly

1st time, both hands 8va higher

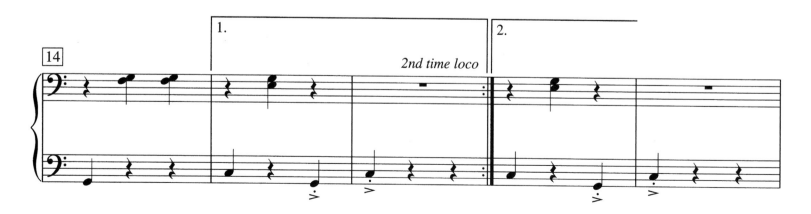

CHOPSTICKS

By ARTHUR DE LULLI

PRIMO

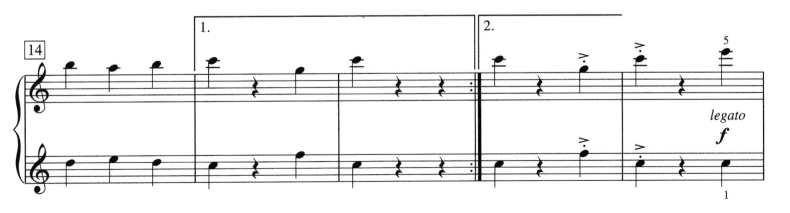

HEART AND SOUL
from the Paramount Short Subject A SONG IS BORN

SECONDO

Words by FRANK LOESSER
Music by HOAGY CARMICHAEL

HEART AND SOUL

from the Paramount Short Subject A SONG IS BORN

PRIMO

Words by FRANK LOESSER
Music by HOAGY CARMICHAEL

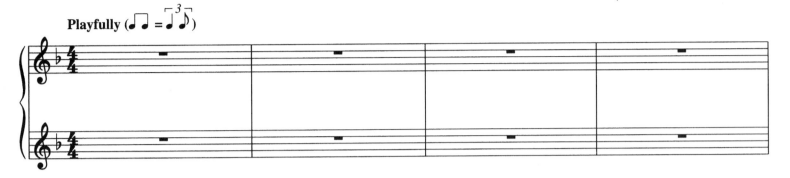

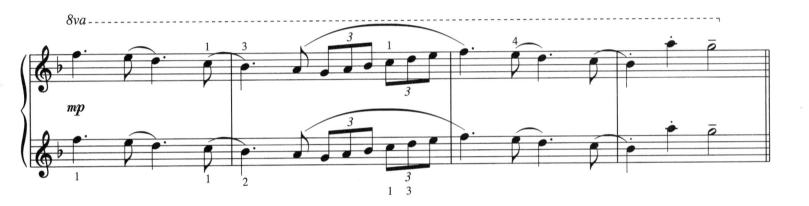

SECONDO

PRIMO

SECONDO

MUSIC! MUSIC! MUSIC!
(Put Another Nickel In)

Words and Music by STEPHAN WEISS
and BERNIE BAUM

SECONDO

MUSIC! MUSIC! MUSIC!
(Put Another Nickel In)

Words and Music by STEPHAN WEISS
and BERNIE BAUM

PRIMO

With gusto

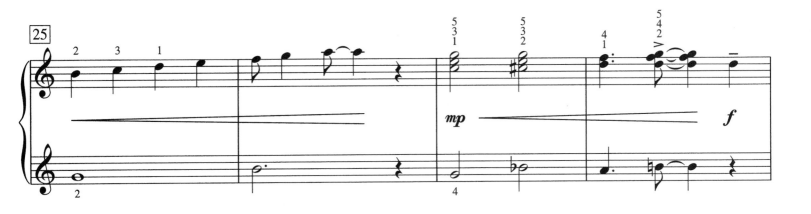

ON TOP OF SPAGHETTI

SECONDO

Words and Music by
TOM GLAZER

ON TOP OF SPAGHETTI

PRIMO

Words and Music by
TOM GLAZER

RAIDERS MARCH

from the Paramount Motion Picture RAIDERS OF THE LOST ARK

SECONDO

Music by
JOHN WILLIAMS

March tempo

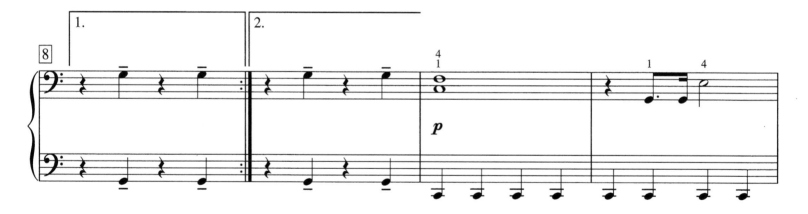

RAIDERS MARCH

from the Paramount Motion Picture RAIDERS OF THE LOST ARK

PRIMO

Music by
JOHN WILLIAMS

THE RAINBOW CONNECTION

from THE MUPPET MOVIE

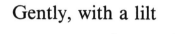

Words and Music by PAUL WILLIAMS
and KENNETH L. ASCHER

Gently, with a lilt

THE RAINBOW CONNECTION

from THE MUPPET MOVIE

PRIMO

Words and Music by PAUL WILLIAMS
and KENNETH L. ASCHER

Gently, with a lilt

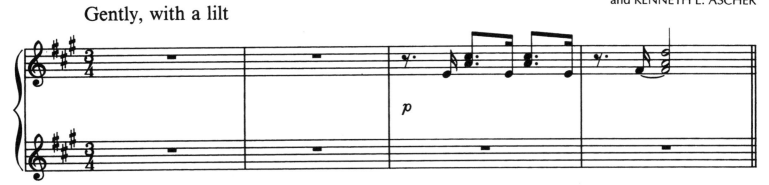

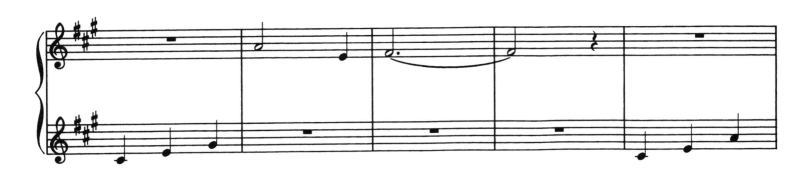

SECONDO

PRIMO

SECONDO

PRIMO

SECONDO

PRIMO

SECONDO

PRIMO

Y.M.C.A.

SECONDO

Words and Music by JACQUES MORALI,
HENRY BELOLO and VICTOR WILLIS

With a Disco beat

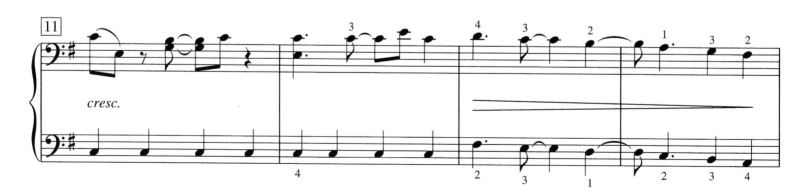

Y.M.C.A.

PRIMO

Words and Music by JACQUES MORALI,
HENRY BELOLO and VICTOR WILLIS

With a Disco beat

SECONDO

PIANO FOR TWO
A Variety of Piano Duets from Hal Leonard

ADELE FOR PIANO DUET
Intermediate Level

Eight of Adele's biggest hits arranged especially for intermediate piano duet! Featuring: Chasing Pavements • Hello • Make You Feel My Love • Rolling in the Deep • Set Fire to the Rain • Skyfall • Someone Like You • When We Were Young.

00172162 1 Piano, 4 Hands.............................$14.99

THE BEATLES FOR PIANO DUET
Intermediate Level
arr. Eric Baumgartner

Eight great Beatles' songs arranged for piano duet! Titles: Blackbird • Come Together • In My Life • Lucy in the Sky with Diamonds • Michelle • Ob-la-di, Ob-la-da • While My Guitar Gently Weeps • Yellow Submarine.

00275877 1 Piano, 4 Hands $14.99

THE BIG BOOK OF PIANO DUETS

24 great piano duet arrangements! Includes: Beauty and the Beast • Clocks • Edelweiss • Georgia on My Mind • He's a Pirate • Let It Go • Linus and Lucy • Moon River • Yellow Submarine • You are the Sunshine of My Life • and more!

00232851 1 Piano, 4 Hands.............................$17.99

CONTEMPORARY DISNEY DUETS
Intermediate Level

8 great Disney duets: Evermore (from Beauty and the Beast) • How Does a Moment Last Forever (from Beauty and the Beast) • How Far I'll Go (from Moana) • Lava • Let It Go (from Frozen) • Proud Corazon (from Coco) • Remember Me (from Coco) • You're Welcome (from Moana).

00285562 1 Piano, 4 Hands.............................$12.99

EASY CLASSICAL DUETS
 Book/Online Audio
Willis Music

7 great piano duets to perform at a recital, play-for-fun, or sightread: By the Beautiful Blue Danube (Strauss) • Eine kleine Nachtmusik (Mozart) • Hungarian Rhapsody No. 5 (Liszt) • Morning from Peer Gynt (Grieg) • Rondeau (Mouret) • Sleeping Beauty Waltz (Tchaikovsky) • Surprise Symphony (Haydn). Includes online audio tracks for the primo and secondo part for download or streaming.

00145767 1 Piano, 4 Hands.............................$12.99

FAVORITE DISNEY SONGS FOR PIANO DUET
Early Intermediate Level

8 great Disney songs creatively arranged for piano duet: Can You Feel the Love Tonight • Do You Want to Build a Snowman • A Dream Is a Wish Your Heart Makes • Supercalifragilisticexpialidocious • That's How You Know • When Will My Life Begin? • You'll Be in My Heart • You've Got a Friend in Me.

00285563 1 Piano, 4 Hands.............................$14.99

FIRST 50 PIANO DUETS YOU SHOULD PLAY

Includes: Autumn Leaves • Bridge over Troubled Water • Chopsticks • Fields of Gold • Hallelujah • Imagine • Lean on Me • Theme from "New York, New York" • Over the Rainbow • Peaceful Easy Feeling • Singin' in the Rain • A Thousand Years • What the World Needs Now Is Love • You Raise Me Up • and more.

00276571 1 Piano, 4 Hands.............................$19.99

GOSPEL DUETS
The Phillip Keveren Series

Eight inspiring hymns arranged by Phillip Keveren for one piano, four hands, including: Church in the Wildwood • His Eye Is on the Sparrow • In the Garden • Just a Closer Walk with Thee • The Old Rugged Cross • Shall We Gather at the River? • There Is Power in the Blood • When the Roll Is Called up Yonder.

00295099 1 Piano, 4 Hands.............................$12.99

THE GREATEST SHOWMAN
by Benj Pasek & Justin Paul
Intermediate Level

Creative piano duet arrangements for the songs: Come Alive • From Now On • The Greatest Show • A Million Dreams • Never Enough • The Other Side • Rewrite the Stars • This Is Me • Tightrope.

00295078 1 Piano, 4 Hands............................. $16.99

BILLY JOEL FOR PIANO DUET
Intermediate Level

8 of the Piano Man's greatest hits – perfect as recital encores, or just for fun! Titles: It's Still Rock and Roll to Me • Just the Way You Are • The Longest Time • My Life • New York State of Mind • Piano Man • She's Always a Woman • Uptown Girl.

00141139 1 Piano, 4 Hands.............................$14.99

HEART AND SOUL & OTHER DUET FAVORITES

8 fun duets arranged for two people playing on one piano. Includes: Any Dream Will Do • Chopsticks • Heart and Soul • Music! Music! Music! (Put Another Nickel In) • On Top of Spaghetti • Raiders March • The Rainbow Connection • Y.M.C.A..

00290541 1 Piano, 4 Hands.............................$12.99

RHAPSODY IN BLUE
George Gershwin/ arr. Brent Edstrom

Originally written for piano and jazz band, "Rhapsody in Blue" was later orchestrated by Ferde Grofe. This intimate adaptation for piano duet delivers access to advancing pianists and provides an exciting musical collaboration and adventure!

00125150 1 Piano, 4 Hands.............................$14.99

RIVER FLOWS IN YOU & OTHER SONGS FOR PIANO DUET
Intermediate Level

10 great songs including the title song and: All of Me (Piano Guys) • Bella's Lullaby • Beyond • Chariots of Fire • Dawn • Forrest Gump - Main Title (Feather Theme) • Primavera • Somewhere in Time • Watermark.

00141055 1 Piano, 4 Hands.............................$12.99

TOP HITS FOR EASY PIANO DUET
 Book/Online Audio
arr. David Pearl

10 great songs with backing tracks: Despacito (Justin Bieber ft. Luis Fonsi & Daddy Yankee) • Havana (Camila Cabello ft. Young Thug • High Hopes (Panic! At the Disco) • A Million Dreams (The Greatest Showman) • Perfect (Ed Sheeran) • Senorita (Camila Cabello & Shawn Mendes) • Shallow (Lady Gaga & Bradley Cooper) • Someone You Loved (Lewis Capaldi) • Speechless (Aladdin) • Sucker (Jonas Brothers).

00326133 1 Piano, 4 Hands.............................$12.99

HAL•LEONARD®
www.halleonard.com

EASY PIANO PLAY-ALONGS
Orchestrated arrangements with you as the soloist!

This series lets you play along with great accompaniments to songs you know and love! Each book comes with recordings of complete professional performances and includes matching custom arrangements in easy piano format. With these books you can: Listen to complete professional performances of each of the songs; Play the easy piano arrangements along with the performances; Sing along with the recordings; Play the easy piano arrangements as solos, without the audio.

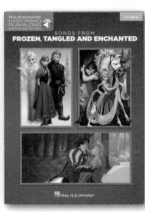

1. GREAT JAZZ STANDARDS
00310916 Book/CD Pack...........................$14.95

2. FAVORITE CLASSICAL THEMES
00310921 Book/CD Pack...........................$14.95

3. BROADWAY FAVORITES
00310915 Book/CD Pack...........................$14.95

4. ADELE
00156223 Book/Online Audio..................$16.99

5. HIT POP/ROCK BALLADS
00310917 Book/CD Pack...........................$14.95

6. LOVE SONG FAVORITES
00310918 Book/CD Pack...........................$14.95

7. O HOLY NIGHT
00310920 Book/CD Pack...........................$14.95

9. COUNTRY BALLADS
00311105 Book/CD Pack...........................$14.95

11. DISNEY BLOCKBUSTERS
00311107 Book/Online Audio..................$14.99

12. CHRISTMAS FAVORITES
00311257 Book/CD Pack...........................$14.95

13. CHILDREN'S SONGS
00311258 Book/CD Pack...........................$14.95

15. DISNEY'S BEST
00311260 Book/Online Audio.................$16.99

16. LENNON & MCCARTNEY HITS
00311262 Book/CD Pack...........................$14.95

17. HOLIDAY HITS
00311329 Book/CD Pack...........................$14.95

18. WEST SIDE STORY
00130739 Book/Online Audio $14.99

19. TAYLOR SWIFT
00142735 Book/Online Audio $14.99

**20. ANDREW LLOYD WEBBER –
FAVORITES**
00311775 Book/CD Pack...........................$14.99

21. GREAT CLASSICAL MELODIES
00311776 Book/CD Pack...........................$14.99

22. ANDREW LLOYD WEBBER – HITS
00311785 Book/CD Pack...........................$14.99

23. DISNEY CLASSICS
00311836 Book/CD Pack...........................$14.99

24. LENNON & MCCARTNEY FAVORITES
00311837 Book/CD Pack...........................$14.99

26. WICKED
00311882 Book/CD Pack...........................$16.99

27. THE SOUND OF MUSIC
00311897 Book/Online Audio.................$14.99

28. CHRISTMAS CAROLS
00311912 Book/CD Pack...........................$14.99

29. CHARLIE BROWN CHRISTMAS
00311913 Book/CD Pack...........................$14.99

31. STAR WARS
00110283 Book/Online Audio $16.99

**32. SONGS FROM FROZEN, TANGLED
AND ENCHANTED**
00126896 Book/Online Audio $14.99

Disney characters and artwork © Disney Enterprises, Inc.

*Prices, contents and availability subject
to change without notice.*

FOR MORE INFORMATION, SEE YOUR LOCAL MUSIC DEALER,
OR WRITE TO:

HAL•LEONARD®
C O R P O R A T I O N
7777 W. BLUEMOUND RD. P.O. BOX 13819 MILWAUKEE, WI 53213

www.halleonard.com

0516